for Kids

Cats

DAWN TITMUS

BROWN BEAR BOOKS

Published by Brown Bear Books Ltd
Unit 1/D, Leroy House
436 Essex Road
London N1 3QP

ISBN 978 1 78121 460 2

For Brown Bear Books Ltd:
Text and editor: Dawn Titmus
Editorial Director: Lindsey Lowe
Children's Publisher: Anne O'Daly
Design Manager: Keith Davis
Picture Manager: Sophie Mortimer

Picture Credits
t=top, c=centre, b=bottom, l=left, r=right
Interior: I23rf: Anna Yakimova 8; iStock: 101cats 20–21, 2002 lubava1981 5, Angelika 18b, bruev 29br, Axel
Bueckert 24–25, FatCamera 4, fotoedu 16–17, FrankvandenBergh 12, Highwaystrarz_Photography 17, kmsh
7c, Valery Kudryavstev 14, lopurice 9c, MyImages_Micha 15b, Okissi68 16, Alona Rjabceva 21t, RyersonClark
10, Seregraff 29bl, Sergeeva 29t, Dimitri Surkov 25b, SVM 27b; Shutterstock: Africa Studio 7b, Ermolaev
Alexander 12–13, 14–15, Maxim Blinkov 27t, Axel Bueckert 15t, Chengongshan 19b, chromstos 25t, Foonia
6, Happy Monkey 23t, Eric Isselee 1, 4–5, 22–23, Kristaps K 19t, kurhan 8–9, Maggy Meyer 18t, Millenius 9t,
Okssi 11, onnixxino 13t, Tatyana Panova 26–27, Anurak Pongpatimet 21b, siraphat 7tr, Yuliia Sonsedska 3,
10–11 Julie Vader 13c, VaLiza 23b, Yellow Cat 7tl.
All other photos and artwork, Brown Bear Books.

Brown Bear Books has made every attempt to contact the copyright holder.
If anyone has any information please contact licensing@brownbearbooks.co.uk

A catalogue record for this book is available from the British Library

Printed in Malaysia

Contents

Which cat?

Owning and looking after a cat is great fun and very rewarding. A happy cat makes for an affectionate pet. Whether you live in a city or in the country, a cat will adapt well to most people's lifestyles.

Rescue a cat

Looking after a kitten takes time and energy. Rescue centres are full of adult cats that need new homes. Think about giving an older cat from a rescue centre a forever home. Look for a healthy cat with clear, bright eyes, a glossy coat and no signs of sickness.

Buying a kitten

Kittens should stay with their mothers until they are about 14 weeks old. Buy directly from a breeder if you want a pedigree kitten. Check out notices for kittens at the vet and in the local paper. Ask friends and neighbours if they know of local litters.

The right cat for you?

☑ Will the cat have access to a safe outside area, such as a garden?

☑ Indoor cats need activities and toys so they don't get bored. Do you have the time to play with your cat every day?

☑ Do you have the time to groom a cat? Long-haired cats, especially, need lots of grooming.

☑ Can your family afford the food costs and vet bills?

Read on ...

Cats are great companions and are less demanding than other pets, but it is important to choose the right one. This book will help you to pick and care for your pet. Learn about four of the most popular breeds. Try your hand at making a fun cat toy. You will also find some fascinating facts about your furry friend!

What you will need

All cats need some basic items, such as food and water bowls, a collar with identification (ID) tag and some toys. Your cat will also need a bed to sleep in.

What you need

- ✓ Food and water bowls the right size for your cat.

- ✓ Collar with ID tag. Some cats will walk on a lead.

- ✓ Grooming brushes and comb.

- ✓ Litter tray and litter if your cat doesn't have access to the outside.

- ✓ Toys, such as balls and catnip mice, and a scratching post or pad.

- ✓ Bed and a cat carrier.

Cat carrier

You'll need a pet carrier to take your cat on car journeys or to go to the vet. A nervous cat loose in a moving car may distract the driver. Putting the cat in a carrier is safer and helps your cat to feel more secure.

Grooming

All cats need some brushing. Some long-haired cats need grooming every day. You will need a soft brush and a comb especially for your cat.

← Double-sided grooming brush

Litter tray

If your cat cannot go outside to go to the toilet, it will need a litter tray with a scoop and some cat litter.

 Litter tray

Playtime

All cats need to play to keep them fit and healthy. Playing with your cat can also create a stronger bond between you. There are many different cat toys in the pet shop, or you can make your own. Scratching pads and posts help protect furniture in the home.

Cat collars

Use a safety collar that pulls off easily if the cat gets it caught on something. Many collars have a bell to warn birds of nearby cats!

← Collar with bell

Feeding time

Your cat needs the right amount of food every day to keep it fit and healthy. It also needs clean drinking water. The amount to feed your cat depends on its size, its age and its activity.

How much to feed

The guide on your cat's food tin or packet shows how much to feed your cat. Make sure you measure out the right amount. Check your cat's weight every month. If your cat is gaining or losing weight, adjust the amount of food and treats you give it.

Cat food

Tinned food comes in a wide range of flavours, but some people don't like the smell. A good way to give your cat a balanced diet is to feed it a high-quality complete dry food. Dry food can be left out all day so your cat can eat when it likes. Watch that your cat doesn't overeat!

Tasty titbits

Give your cat some home-cooked food occasionally as a treat. Give them a small amount of tuna, cooked chicken or cooked scrambled eggs. You can also buy special cat treats from a supermarket or pet shop.

Water bowls

In the wild, cats don't drink water near animals they have killed for food. Their instincts tell them the water may be poisoned by the food. Many house cats don't like to drink water right next to their food for the same reason.

Watch out!

Never feed dog food to your cat. It doesn't have the right nutrients for cats. When a kitten has been weaned, don't give it milk. Milk can cause diarrhoea in some cats.

Grooming and cleaning

Most cats groom their coats every day unless they are in pain or unwell. Grooming keeps the coat clean and removes loose hair. Help your cat keep its coat clean and tangle-free by grooming it regularly.

Healthy teeth

Just like people, cats need clean, healthy teeth. If possible, start cleaning your cat's teeth when it is a kitten. Ask an adult to help you. You will need special toothpaste made for cats – don't use ordinary toothpaste. You can use an extra-soft toothbrush, a finger brush or a piece of cloth. If your cat is not used to having its teeth cleaned, it's best to ask the vet to do it until it is used to the idea.

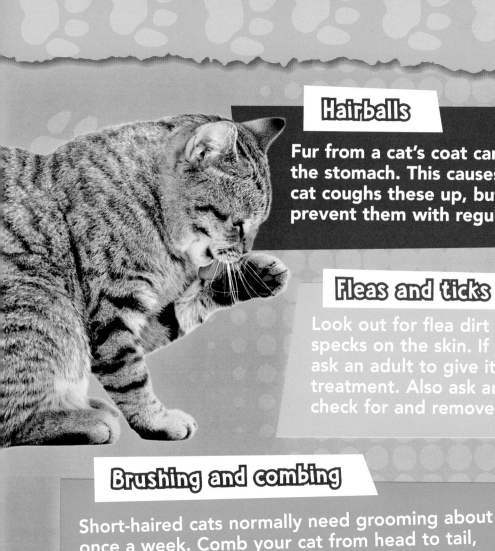

Hairballs

Fur from a cat's coat can build up in the stomach. This causes hairballs. Your cat coughs these up, but you can help prevent them with regular grooming.

Fleas and ticks

Look out for flea dirt – small, dark specks on the skin. If your cat has fleas, ask an adult to give it some antiflea treatment. Also ask an adult to help check for and remove any ticks.

Brushing and combing

Short-haired cats normally need grooming about once a week. Comb your cat from head to tail, and then use a bristle brush on its coat. Many long-haired cats need daily grooming or their fur can become matted. Use a wide-tooth comb or slicker brush to gently tease out any tangles. Take care not to pull too hard and hurt your cat. Use a bristle brush for the tail. Spray-on conditioner can help smooth out any tangles.

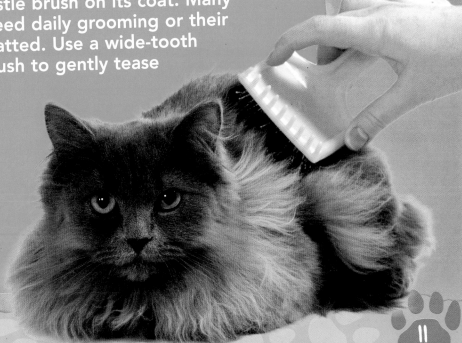

Exercise

When they are not sleeping, cats love to have something to do. Cats that are outside much of the time get plenty of exercise. Cats that live inside need more activities to stop them getting bored.

Playtime

Most cats love to play. Kittens need lots of playtime every day. It helps them practise adult behaviour, and builds strength and coordination. Give your cat some fun toys that you can play with together. You can also make your own toys. Cut holes in a cardboard box for your cat to jump inside and hide. Give it rolled-up newspaper balls to play with. You can build a fun zone for your cat with boxes, perching areas, ropes to climb and tunnels to run through.

Cat toys

Outside cats

If your cat spends most of its time outdoors, it is free to roam, run, climb and chase birds and mice. It will get all the exercise it needs.

Cat flap

A pet door can be useful if no one is at home during the day to let the cat in and out. A door allows your cat to come and go as it pleases. Make sure the pet door is the right size and height for your kitty!

Older cats

Older cats may have problems with hearing and eyesight, which can make it less safe for them to exercise outdoors. They also spend more time sleeping than playing, so they need to eat less food than before. Play gently with an older cat indoors. It needs to be kept active even when it gets older.

Training

Some natural cat behaviour can become a problem for owners, such as clawing furniture. Train your cat to be a well-behaved member of the family.

House-training a kitten

Learn the signs that your kitten wants to go to the toilet. Put the kitten in the litter tray immediately it shows the signs, when it wakes up and after meals. Reward the behaviour with praise or a titbit. Never punish a kitten for going to the toilet in the wrong place. Just pick it up and put it in the litter tray. Clean up the soiled area to stop the kitten using the same place again.

Rewards

You can use treats, toys, praise or play as rewards for good behaviour.

Good manners

Good manners can be taught through reward and praise. Encourage your cat to sit still for grooming by giving it a titbit. If your cat likes to nibble houseplants, offer it something else to eat such as dried food. To stop problem behaviour, say 'No!' firmly. Never shout at your cat or punish it.

Ask the vet

A cat that fights or is aggressive towards other pets or animals may be stressed or sick. If your cat likes to fight, your vet can give advice about what to do.

Scratching post

Cats that spend most of their time outside sharpen their claws on trees and fence posts. Indoor cats may scratch the furniture, carpets or curtains instead. Give your cat a scratch pad or scratching post to prevent damage to furniture.

Scratching post

Staying healthy

You can help your cat stay healthy by keeping its jabs up to date and making sure it gets healthy food and enough exercise. Even so, just like people, cats get sick sometimes.

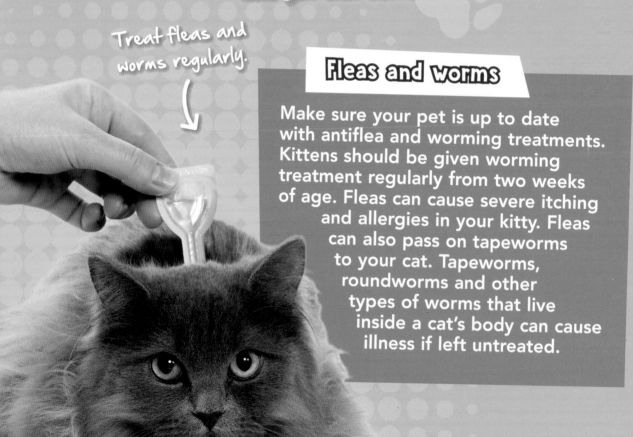

Treat fleas and worms regularly.

Fleas and worms

Make sure your pet is up to date with antiflea and worming treatments. Kittens should be given worming treatment regularly from two weeks of age. Fleas can cause severe itching and allergies in your kitty. Fleas can also pass on tapeworms to your cat. Tapeworms, roundworms and other types of worms that live inside a cat's body can cause illness if left untreated.

16

A visit to the vet

Take your cat to the vet once a year for its booster jabs and a check-up. You will need a pet carrier to transport your pet. Your vet will ask questions about your cat's general health and any problems it may have.

Coat and skin

When you groom your cat, look for rough or red patches of skin. Check for bald or thinning patches on its coat. The vet can treat skin and coat problems with medicine.

Jabs

Kittens should be vaccinated against disease when they are about eight weeks old. They will need a second set of shots when they are three months old. Keep your kitten inside until it has had the full vaccination programme. Adult cats need booster jabs every year.

In the wild

Domestic cats often behave in the same way as wild cats. They hunt prey and bring it home, and they like a high perch for sleeping.

Big cats

Leopards (right) belong to the same family as domestic cats. The cat family also includes lions, tigers, cheetahs and pumas. All cats eat meat, and they have claws that they use to grip their prey. Most cats in the wild hunt alone, rather than in packs.

African wildcat

Scientists have discovered that all domestic cats today descend from a type of African wildcat. It lives in North Africa and the Near East. The African wildcat lives alone. It hunts its prey at dawn and at dusk. It sleeps a lot and likes to sleep high off the ground in trees.

First pet cats

Cats probably began to be domesticated about 9,000 years ago. At that time, early farmers in the Near East began to store grain. The grain attracted rats and mice. They attracted cats. People realized that cats were good at keeping rats and mice under control. That was the start of people and cats living together.

The sociable cat

Domestic cats can develop strong bonds with people and other household pets. In the wild, some cats live in groups that work together. Lions live in family groups called prides, with up to 20 or 30 members.

Persian

The Persian is a popular breed all around the world. It is quiet and affectionate. Also known as the Persian longhair, it has a very long, soft, silky coat.

The Persian is a sweet, playful cat.

Where in the world?

The Persian probably comes from Persia (modern Iran) and Turkey. Persian cats were imported into Europe (France and Italy) in 1620. Persians were shown at the first ever cat show in the United Kingdom in 1871.

Breed profile

The Persian is a large, solidly built long-haired cat. It is famous for its flat face and large eyes. An adult Persian weighs about 4 to 7 kg. The coat comes in many colours, including black, white, blue, red, cream and silver tabby. Persians usually live for about 13 to 15 years.

Looking after me

The Persian is a gentle, calm cat that loves to be around people.

- ☑ Persians like to stay indoors and adapt well to living in a flat.

- ☑ The long coat tangles easily and needs to be groomed every day to prevent matting.

Maine Coon

The Maine Coon comes from the United States. It is becoming more and more popular in the United Kingdom. It is a gentle giant, with a friendly, easygoing nature. It has a thick, shaggy coat. Its tail is at least as long as its body.

Where in the world?

The cat gets its name from the state of Maine in northeast United States. There are many stories about where it came from. The most likely story is that longhair cats brought from Europe mated with local short-haired cats to produce the Maine Coon.

The Maine Coon is the largest domestic cat breed.

Breed profile

Maine Coons are large, handsome cats. Males can weigh up to 8 kg. Females are usually smaller at up to 5.5 kg. There is a wide range of colours. The tail is long and bushy with rings like a raccoon's tail. The Maine Coon lives for about 12 to 15 years.

Looking after me

The Maine Coon is a playful cat. It needs plenty of space and access to the outside.

- ✔ Although it has a thick coat, it does not need daily grooming.

- ✔ Unlike most cats, the Maine Coon can be taught simple tricks such as fetching things. It can also be taught to walk on a lead.

Siamese

Siamese are affectionate, intelligent cats. They like to be around people and often have a strong bond with one person. They have a loud miaow, which can sound like a baby crying.

The Siamese is a clever, curious cat.

Where in the world?

Siamese cats guarded the royal temples in Siam (modern Thailand). Legend says that only members of the royal family could own them. Siamese cats were brought to the United Kingdom in the 1880s and quickly became popular.

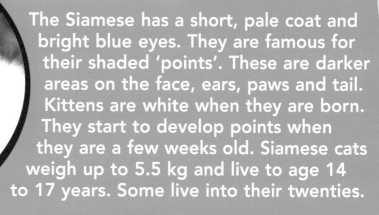

Breed profile

The Siamese has a short, pale coat and bright blue eyes. They are famous for their shaded 'points'. These are darker areas on the face, ears, paws and tail. Kittens are white when they are born. They start to develop points when they are a few weeks old. Siamese cats weigh up to 5.5 kg and live to age 14 to 17 years. Some live into their twenties.

Looking after me

Siamese cats are very social and should not be left alone for long.

☑ Siamese can live in flats but they also like large houses with gardens. They are suitable for families with children.

☑ Siamese are very intelligent and can be trained to come when their name is called.

Abyssinian

The Abyssinian is one of the top five most popular breeds in the world. It is a muscular cat with a thick, golden coat, slender legs and small, oval feet.

Where in the world?

No one is sure where the Abyssinian came from. One story says that British soldiers took these cats to Europe from Abyssinia (modern Ethiopia) in the 1860s. The first cat known to be Abyssinian came to the United Kingdom in 1868.

The Abyssinian needs lots of company.

Breed profile

Abyssinians are known for their patterned coat and beautiful face markings. They come in a range of colours but are usually golden-brown with black bands on the individual hairs, known as ticking. The cats weigh about 4.5 kg. They live to age 14 to 16 years.

Looking after me

The Abyssinian likes to be around people but prefers not to be part of a group of cats.

- ☑ It is gentle with children and makes an ideal family pet.

- ☑ It is intelligent and playful, and can be trained to do tricks.

Make it !
Make a cat toy

You can make this simple toy for your cat
to play with. Fill it with treats your cat loves.
It will enjoy working out how to get at the treats!

You will need:

A large empty tissue box

Ribbon or string

About 14 toilet roll tubes

Glue

Cat treats

4 Tie the box to a piece of furniture so it does not move around.

5 Fill some of the tubes with treats that your cat loves.

Sit back and watch your cat have fun exploring the tubes to get at the tasty treats!

1 Ask an adult to make two small holes in the back of the tissue box.

2 Thread the ribbon or string through the holes so that the box can be attached to a solid object such as a table leg.

3 Glue the tubes together and to the inside of the box. Start by gluing tubes along one of the longest sides of the box. Then add a middle row of tubes and finish with a top layer of tubes. Make sure the tubes are firmly glued together and to the box.

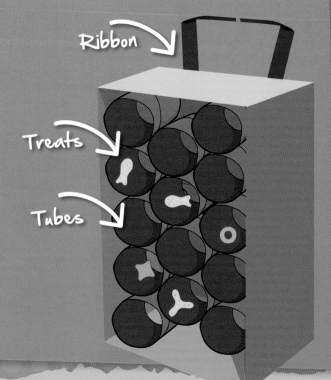

Ribbon

Treats

Tubes

Did you know?

There are about 8 million pet cats in the United Kingdom. About 17 percent of UK households own a cat.

A group of cats is called a clowder.

An ancient Egyptian goddess called Bastet had a cat's head.

Cats purr not only when they are content but also when they are nervous.

There are more than 500 million pet cats in the world.

Cats have excellent night vision. They can see at light levels six times lower than a human needs in order to be able to see.

A cat's whiskers are very sensitive. When a cat brushes its whiskers against an object, it can tell the size and location of the object, even in the dark!

Cat organizations recognize about 40 breeds of cats. About one new breed is added every year.

Cats can't taste sweet things because they don't have taste buds that can detect sugar.

Cats sleep on average for about 13 to 14 hours a day. A 10-year-old child needs about 10 hours sleep every night.

Glossary

breed (1) to take care of a group of animals to produce more animals of a particular kind. (2) a particular kind of animal that has been produced by breeding.

breeder person who breeds certain animals, such as cats.

domestic living with people.

flea very small biting insect that lives on animals.

house-train to train an animal to go to the toilet outside or in the correct place.

ID tag short for 'identification' tag and worn on the pet's collar.

instinct way of behaving that is not learned, natural behaviour.

jabs see **vaccination**

litter (1) dry material placed in a litter tray. (2) group of young animals born at the same time to the same mother.

nutrient substance that animals need to live and grow.

pedigree history of an animal's parents, showing it is pure-bred.

prey animal hunted by another for food.

pure-bred animal bred from parents of the same breed.

roundworm small, round worm that lives in the stomachs of animals and people.

slicker brush brush with fine wire pins for untangling hair.

tapeworm long, flat worm that lives in the stomachs of animals and people.

tick very small insect that attaches itself to a larger animal and feeds on it.

vaccination treatment with a substance, called a vaccine, to protect against a particular disease.

weaned feed an animal food other than its mother's milk.

Further resources

Books

Caring for Cats and Kittens, Ben Hubbard
(Franklin Watts, 2015)

How to Speak Cat: A Guide to Decoding Cat Language,
Aline Alexander and Gary Weitzman
(National Geographic Kids, 2015)

Kitty's Guide to Caring for Your Cat (Pets' Guides),
Anita Ganeri (Raintree, 2014)

Websites

www.cats.org.uk/cat-care/cats-for-kids/about-cats
Visit the website of the Cat Protection charity for
information about how to care for your pet cat.

**www.rspca.org.uk/adviceandwelfare/pets/cats/
kittens/kittencare**
Advice from the RSPCA on how to look after a kitten.

**http://www.sciencekids.co.nz/sciencefacts/
animals/cat.html**
Lots of interesting facts about cats and kittens.

Index